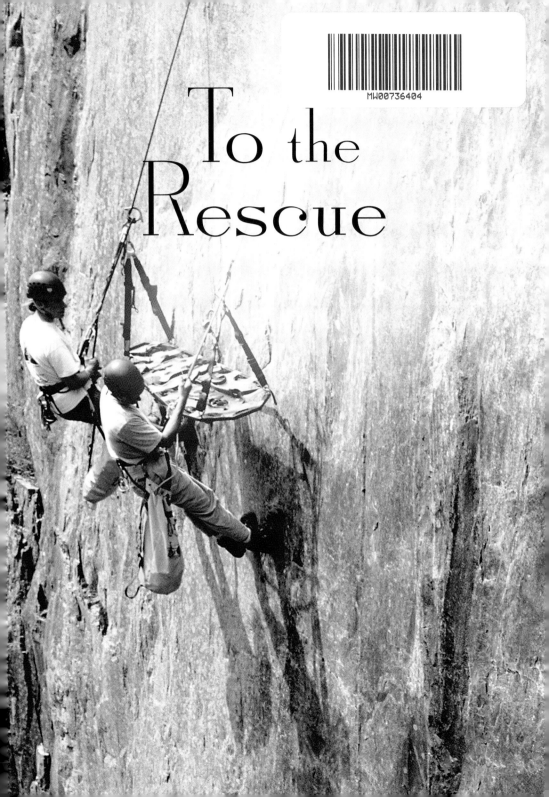

To the Rescue

Contents

Features

Do you know the name of the special tool firefighters use to free people trapped in car wrecks? Check it out on page 10.

In a violent storm at sea, the crew on a sinking ship sent a signal for help. Follow the exciting story in **Coast Guard Heroes** on page 18.

Atlantic puffin chicks sometimes get lost on their way to sea. You can read how children help them find their way in **Puffin Protectors** on page 24.

How can robots rescue people from beneath fallen buildings? To find out, turn to page 26.

How would you act in an earthquake?

Visit www.rigbyinfoquest.com
for more about RESCUE.

Lives on the Line

Imagine being lost and alone on a cold, dark night. Suddenly, you see the warm glow of a flashlight and a rescue party appears. You are safe!

Around the world, brave people do all that they can to rescue people and animals in danger. Some people put their lives on the line every day to rescue others. They work in the emergency rescue services. Because they are the first at the scene of an emergency, they often face great danger. They need to be highly trained and strong enough to handle any **disaster**.

As well as having medical training, many rescue workers have special skills in **mountaineering** or deep-sea diving.

First at the Scene

Medical Rescue

Ambulance workers are called **paramedics**. They are usually the first rescue workers to arrive at an emergency. They provide emergency medical care while the patient is being rushed to a hospital.

Paramedics often work in difficult conditions. They sometimes rescue people trapped in cars or lying injured on the roadside. Ambulances carry lifesaving gear. Flashing lights and sirens warn people that they are coming.

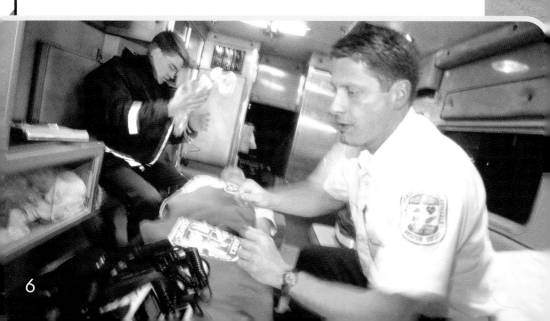

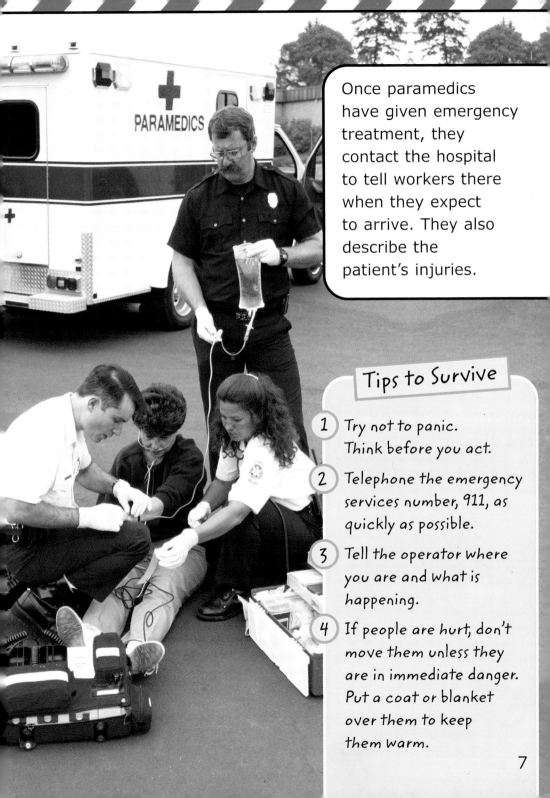

Once paramedics have given emergency treatment, they contact the hospital to tell workers there when they expect to arrive. They also describe the patient's injuries.

Tips to Survive

1. Try not to panic. Think before you act.

2. Telephone the emergency services number, 911, as quickly as possible.

3. Tell the operator where you are and what is happening.

4. If people are hurt, don't move them unless they are in immediate danger. Put a coat or blanket over them to keep them warm.

7

Flying Doctors

In crowded cities or wilderness areas, air ambulances are sometimes used to fly sick or injured people to a hospital. Helicopters can fly high above traffic and land on the roofs of buildings. They can fly quickly over rough ground to distant areas that road ambulances cannot reach.

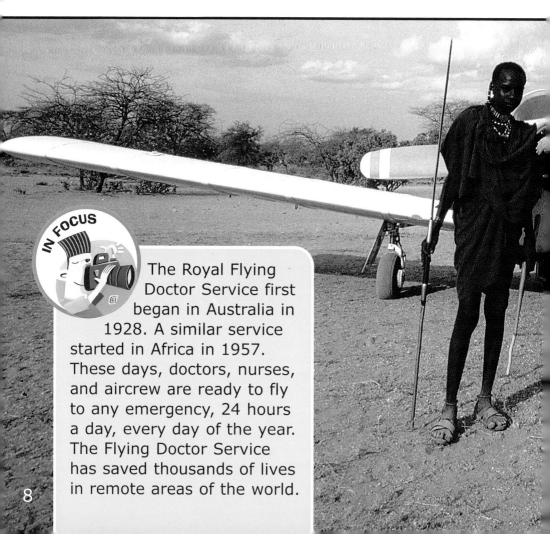

IN FOCUS

The Royal Flying Doctor Service first began in Australia in 1928. A similar service started in Africa in 1957. These days, doctors, nurses, and aircrew are ready to fly to any emergency, 24 hours a day, every day of the year. The Flying Doctor Service has saved thousands of lives in remote areas of the world.

In countries where towns are few and far apart, some doctors travel by plane to medical emergencies. Doctors in parts of Australia and Africa sometimes fly over a thousand miles to make one house call! Pilots often have to land on rough airstrips cut out of the sun-baked desert.

Africa

Nairobi

The Flying Doctor Service in Africa is based in Nairobi, Kenya, and flies to many East African countries.

9

Fighting Fire

Firefighters have one of the most dangerous jobs in the rescue services. When the alarm sounds at the station, the firefighters race to their engines, pulling on protective suits and breathing masks as they go.

WORD BUILDER

Firefighters use special cutters to free people trapped in car crashes. The cutters are called the *jaws of life* and can spread metal or even slice right through it.

Tips to Survive

1. Make sure your home has working smoke alarms.

2. Have an escape plan so that you know the quickest way out in a fire.

3. If your home catches fire, leave immediately.

4. Call 911 and do not go back into the burning building.

At the scene of the fire, one team sprays water onto the fire while another battles through the flames to rescue people trapped inside. Firefighters train to be ready for any crisis, and are often called out to other kinds of emergencies.

Dogs to the Rescue

When people are lost or trapped, special teams of search and rescue dogs and their handlers may be brought in to help. A dog's sense of smell is far better than a human's. A dog can pick up the scent of a missing person from far away or from under heavy snow or rubble.

Search and rescue dogs are specially trained. Their training begins with games of hide-and-seek so that their work becomes fun. The dog and handler build up a strong friendship. The handler learns to understand the dog's signals. A bark may mean "Quick, over here. I've found someone!"

Bailey: Search and Rescue Dog

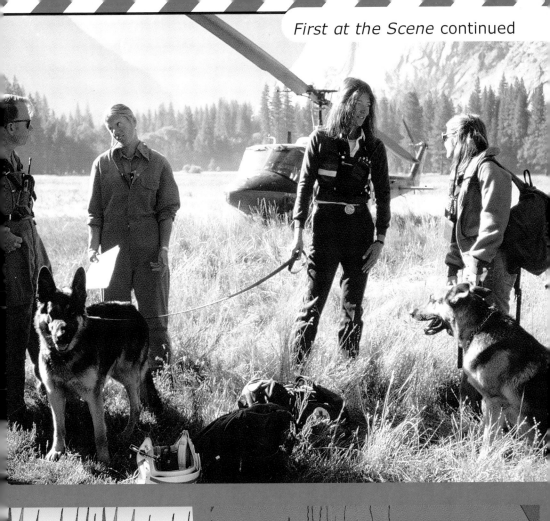

Good job, Bailey!

Everyone has their own special smell. That's how we find lost people.

No problem. It was nothing.

Rescue at Sea

Surf Safe

The sea is fun for swimming, surfing, and boating. But it can also be dangerous. Every year, many swimmers are rescued by lifeguards, usually because they have not followed basic safety rules. Some people swim where it is unsafe, some swim out too far, and some get caught in strong **rips**.

Lifeguards often patrol beaches and are ready to rescue anyone in danger. Sometimes they use lifeboats designed to manage rolling surf.

In Australia and New Zealand, children as young as seven join surf lifesaving clubs. They are taught how to play and swim safely in the surf. They learn basic water safety skills.

Tips to Survive

1. Learn how to swim!
2. Swim between the flags.
3. Observe all warning signs.
4. Never swim alone.
5. Never swim out far.
6. If you get into trouble, don't panic. Float on your back and wave your arm for help.

15

Ocean Rescue

When a boat is missing or people need to be rescued from a sinking vessel, the **coast guard** swings into action. The coast guard can call upon lifeboat crews, helicopters, and long-range aircraft to help rescue people in trouble.

Ocean rescuers use small rubber lifeboats close to shore. Out at sea, large all-weather lifeboats are used. These can roll upright if they **capsize** in bad weather. In the air, rescue helicopters can hover above rough seas and pull people to safety.

Tips to Survive

1. Always wear a life jacket while out boating.

2. Never go boating without an adult and without first checking the weather forecast.

3. Tell someone where you are going and when you expect to be back.

4. If your boat capsizes, do not try to swim for shore. Stay with the boat because it will be easier for rescuers to find you.

Coast Guard Heroes

This true story took place on March 14, 1987, when the U.S. Coast Guard at Cape May, New Jersey, picked up a signal from the Russian freighter *Komsomolets Kirgizii*...

> There's a ship sinking in a violent storm. Thirty-three men, three women, and a baby on board need help immediately.

Within minutes, three helicopters are in the air.

The choppers battle terrible winds and blinding snow to reach the ship.

> It's taken us two hours to get here. We only have enough fuel for another three hours of flying— it's going to be tight!

The terrified crew hold onto the side, watching as the first rescue basket is tossed by the winds.

> I can't hold her steady.

The pilot eases the helicopter closer to the stormy ocean, drags the basket through the waves, and pulls it up the ship's side onto the deck.

Drop the basket into the sea to steady it!

With giant waves hitting them, the crew steady the basket as a woman climbs in with her baby. They are pulled to safety.

She's coming up. Steady, steady. Yes, we've got her!

There's not a moment to spare as the crew, one by one, are pulled up by the helicopters.

The third helicopter lifts the last person to safety. A moment later, the ship sinks. All three helicopters make it back to base.

Spasiba, spasiba! Vie sohranili nasha jizn.

Thank you, thank you! You've saved all our lives.

Mountain Rescue

Mountains can be beautiful one minute and deadly the next. The weather can change quickly, taking climbers and skiers by surprise. There are also dangers from rockfalls and **avalanches.** Rescuers often have to work in blizzards or thick fog to help people who are injured or lost.

Mountain rescuers must be experienced climbers with first-aid training. They work as a team, linked by climbing ropes and carrying ice axes, rope ladders, **flares,** stretchers, and survival bags.

Tips to Survive

1. Check the weather before going into the mountains and always prepare for the worst.

2. Never go into the mountains alone.

3. Tell someone where you are going and when you expect to be back.

4. Only ski in controlled areas.

Animal Rescue

Animals sometimes get lost, injured, or sick and need rescuing, too. Firefighters rescue pets trapped in buildings. People set up shelters to look after abandoned pets until new homes are found. Organizations all over the world work hard to rescue animals in the wild that have been hurt or have lost their homes.

In coastal areas, whales sometimes become stranded on beaches and need help to get back out to sea.

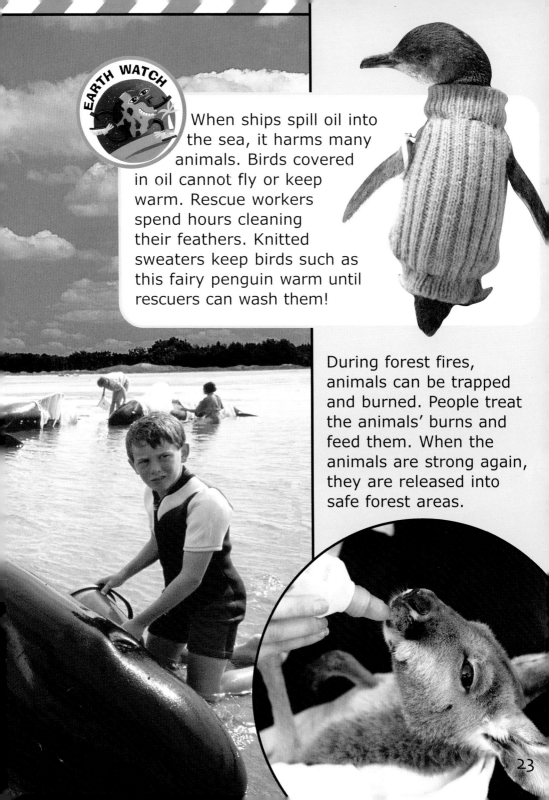

EARTH WATCH

When ships spill oil into the sea, it harms many animals. Birds covered in oil cannot fly or keep warm. Rescue workers spend hours cleaning their feathers. Knitted sweaters keep birds such as this fairy penguin warm until rescuers can wash them!

During forest fires, animals can be trapped and burned. People treat the animals' burns and feed them. When the animals are strong again, they are released into safe forest areas.

Puffin Protectors

Every summer on an island called Heimaey, off Iceland, a special rescue operation takes place. For two weeks, children stay up late into the night rescuing frightened puffins from the streets.

Thousands of Atlantic puffins nest on the island. They dig burrows into the cliffs near town and raise their chicks. When it's time for the chicks to leave home, some get confused by the bright lights of town. Instead of flying out to sea, they land in the streets and panic.

The children search for them with flashlights and gently lift them into boxes. In the morning, they release the birds safely to the sea.

Special Delivery – Safe in the box, a puffin is cycled to the seashore for release.

Iceland

Heimaey

Good Luck Wishes –
A rescued chick is
given a fond farewell.

Taking Flight –
Away from the city
lights, the puffins are
now free.

25

Technology Lifeline

Technology plays an important part in rescue. Special vehicles and gear help with difficult emergencies. Communications technology, such as radar and satellites, locate missing boats and planes. Thermal imaging cameras are searching devices that can detect body heat and find people who are lost or trapped.

Experts predict that by the end of the century, rescue vehicles will be able to hover above people in trouble and lift them directly into the rescue vehicle through a column of air!

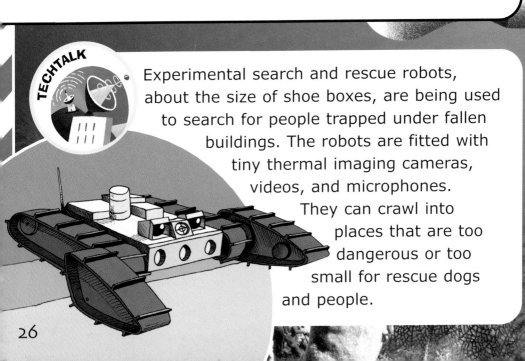

TECHTALK

Experimental search and rescue robots, about the size of shoe boxes, are being used to search for people trapped under fallen buildings. The robots are fitted with tiny thermal imaging cameras, videos, and microphones. They can crawl into places that are too dangerous or too small for rescue dogs and people.

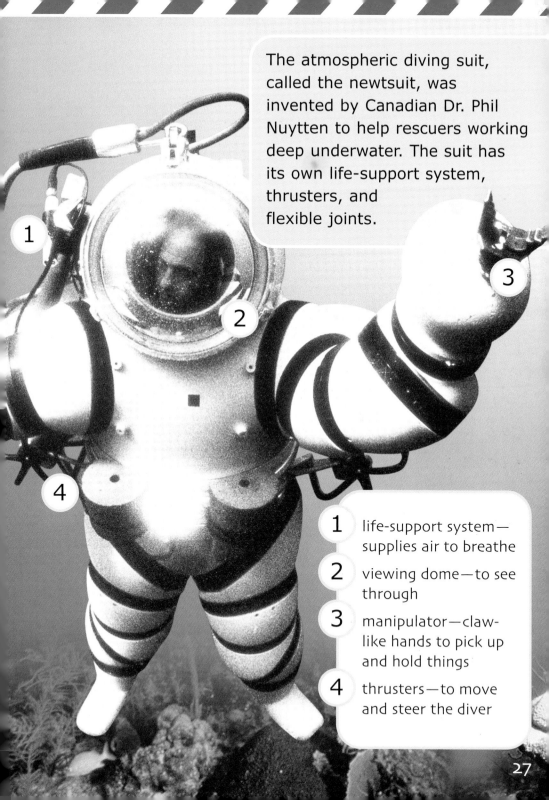

The atmospheric diving suit, called the newtsuit, was invented by Canadian Dr. Phil Nuytten to help rescuers working deep underwater. The suit has its own life-support system, thrusters, and flexible joints.

1 life-support system— supplies air to breathe

2 viewing dome—to see through

3 manipulator—claw-like hands to pick up and hold things

4 thrusters—to move and steer the diver

Survive!

We often learn about amazing stories of rescue and survival. Do you ever wonder how you would act in an emergency? Accidents often happen when we least expect them. Be prepared and learn first aid and map reading. If you do get caught in an emergency, try to remain calm. The brave men, women, and animals of the rescue services will be doing their best to help.

Rescue workers do more than save people's lives. They also teach children how to stay safe and what to do in an emergency.

Be prepared. In a safe place, keep a first-aid kit, and both a flashlight and radio with working batteries. Know how to use a cell phone.

Glossary

avalanche – a mass of snow and ice tumbling down a mountain. An avalanche begins when a block of snow breaks away and slides downhill, collecting more snow as it falls.

capsize – to tip over in the water

coast guard – a branch of the armed forces that watches the sea for ships in danger and protects the country's coastline

disaster – an event that causes great damage, loss, or suffering, such as an earthquake or a serious train wreck

flare – a bright light used as a signal for needing help

mountaineering – the sport or activity of climbing mountains. A mountaineer can rappel, or slide down cliffs and other steep areas using a rope.

paramedic – a person trained to give emergency first aid, but who is not a doctor or nurse

rip – a narrow stretch of fast-flowing, rough water. In a strong rip, a person can be carried out to sea.

Index

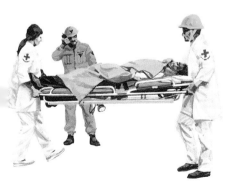

Discussion Starters

1 Fires destroy things in your home. How could you and your family make your home safer from fire? Make an escape plan so you know the quickest way out of your house if there was a fire.

2 People use boats for fishing, waterskiing, sailing, and kayaking. If you could spend a day on a boat, what activity would you most like to do? How would you keep yourself safe on the boat?

3 Of all the rescue workers described in this book, which one would you like to be? Why?